在崩潰前
改寫自己的

命運之書

PICK ME UP

大風文創

PICK ME UP

- SOMETHING TO CHEER YOU UP

- A SELF-AWARE CRY FOR ATTENTION

- LITERALLY HOW TO USE THIS BOOK (OPEN AT RANDOM)

改寫自己的命運之書

- 可以鼓舞人心
- 在你特別渴望受人關心時閱讀
- 閱讀本書的方法（隨意翻開一頁即可）

DEDICATED TO
THE FUTURE

& IN LOVING
MEMORY OF
THE PAST

獻給未來
也是對過去美好回憶的紀念

BUT THAT'S NEVER REALLY STOPPED ME BEFORE

但我未曾因此停下腳步

START (SOMEWHERE)

THIS BOOK IS ALL ABOUT WHO
YOU ARE & WHAT YOU KNOW.

PICK IT UP ANY TIME YOU
NEED SOME DISTRACTION
OR ENCOURAGEMENT.

OPEN TO ANY PAGE NOW &
LEAVE YOUR MARK FOR LATER.
WRITE WITH A CLEAR MIND
THEN RETURN WHEN YOU NEED
SOME OF YOUR OWN ADVICE,
OR A REMINDER OF JUST HOW
MUCH YOU'RE CAPABLE OF.

開始吧（無論從哪一頁都行）⟶

這是一本能讓你了解自己是誰、探索自我內心的書。

當你心煩意亂且需要一些鼓勵時，隨時翻閱這本書吧。

現在，請隨意翻開一頁，在思緒清晰的狀態下記錄此刻的想法。當你需要一些建議時，再回過頭來從自己當下的紀錄中找尋靈感，或許也能從中發現自己是多麼值得肯定。

FIND YOUR WAY BACK
THROUGH THIS JOURNEY
WITH A PAPER TRAIL
ON THE INTERNET.
POST WITH #PICKMEUPBOOK
SO YOU CAN SEARCH LATER.

在閱讀過程中，你可以在網路上留下紀錄，並加上#改寫自己的命運之書的主題標籤，方便你之後快速回顧。

THE ONLY THING
THAT
ACTUALLY
<u>MATTERS</u>

IS BEING HAPPY
WITH WHAT
YOU'VE GOT &
LEARNING TO
MAKE THE
BEST OF IT.

唯一<u>真正重要</u>的事情，
是為自己所擁有的而感到開心，
並學習好好善用這一切。

DESCRIBE YOUR MOOD IN 1 WORD EVERY TIME YOU VISIT THIS PAGE:

每當翻到這一頁時，用一個詞形容當下的心情：

_____   _____

_____   _____

_____   _____

_____   _____

_____   _____

_____   _____

_____   _____

_____   _____

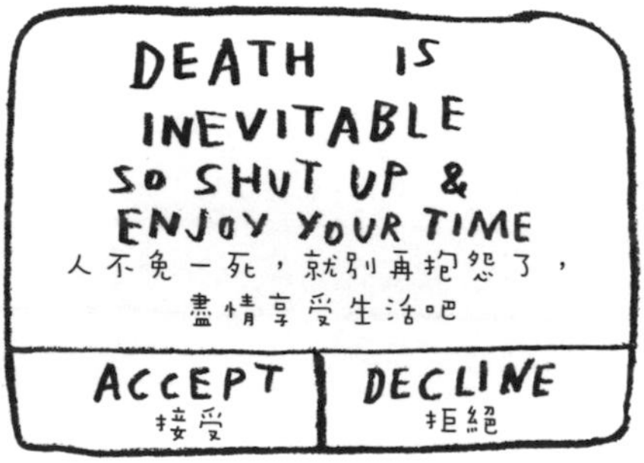
DEATH IS INEVITABLE SO SHUT UP & ENJOY YOUR TIME
人不免一死，就別再抱怨了，
盡情享受生活吧
ACCEPT
接受
DECLINE
拒絕

WHO DO YOU ADMIRE & WHY?
DRAW A PORTRAIT & TAG THEM!

誰是你仰慕的對象？為什麼？
畫下他們的模樣，拍照上傳並標記他們吧！

📷 #PICKMEUPBOOK

WHY ARE YOU SO
PETRIFIED OF SILENCE?
HERE, CAN YOU HANDLE THIS:

為什麼要如此害怕寂靜呢？
現在就來好好面對寂靜：

WRITE SOME GOOD ADVICE

寫下一些好建議

THEN TAKE IT!

接納這些建議吧！

ADMIT IT:

承認吧:

承認它

FEELING SORRY FOR MYSELF

ADMIT ONE

V.I.P. ACCESS

對自己感到抱歉

VIP票

ANXIOUS FOR NO REASON

ADMIT 1

承認它

LIMITED ENGAGE-MENT

莫名焦慮

交流互動太少

STAYING IN & ORDERING A PIZZA

ADMIT ONE

承認它

1 NIGHT ONLY

宅在家,叫外送披薩

VIP票

DRAW SOME
AWARDS NOW,
THEN GIVE THEM
TO YOURSELF
LATER!

現在先畫些獎章吧，
將來再頒發給自己！

EVERYONE HAS VICES.
WE KNOW THEY CAN
BE BAD FOR US, LIKE
CANDY OR BEER, BUT
WE INDULGE ANYWAY.
HELP YOURSELF BY
MAKING THEM TREATS
& NOT THE EXPECTATION.

每個人都有些壞習慣，可能是
愛吃糖果或愛喝啤酒，雖然知
道對自己有害，但還是無法自
拔。把這些惡習當成偶爾給自
己的小獎勵，但不要變成常
態，也許會對你有所幫助。

DESCRIBE THINGS YOU CAN FEEL 描述你用心感受到的事物

BUT NOT EASILY SEE

這些事物常常是眼睛看不見的

IT'S OKAY &
PROBABLY HEALTHY
TO BE "AN OPEN BOOK,"
BUT HANDLE YOURSELF
WITH CARE.

BE GENTLE OR YOU'LL
LOSE YOUR PLACE,
OR WORSE,
CRACK YOUR SPINE.

你可以像「一本攤開的書」般
毫無保留，
但也別忘了保護好自己。

溫柔一點對待自己，
不然你有可能迷失方向，
甚至落得身心俱疲。

ADVICE YOU GAVE RECENTLY THAT YOU MIGHT NEED YOURSELF:

最近給過別人，但也許自己也用得上的建議：

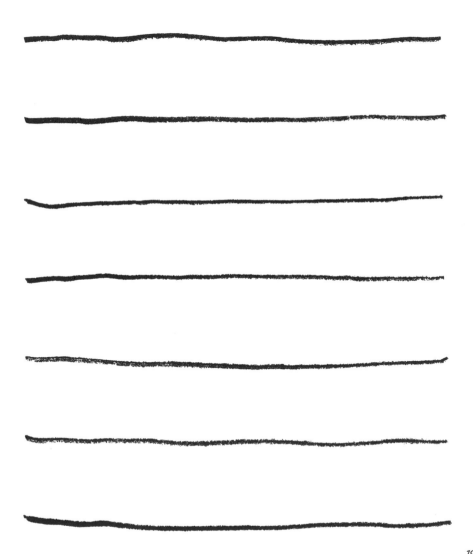

DRAW A BATH ANY
TIME YOU NEED TO
CHILL

需要紓壓放鬆時
就在這裡畫一個浴缸吧！

ADD BANDAGES TO THIS PAGE SO IT DOESN'T FALL APART

為這一頁貼上OK繃，
書頁就不會破裂了

IT CAN BE
SCARY OR HARD
TO BE TRUE TO
YOURSELF.

YOU MAY NEED
TO BIDE YOUR
TIME UNTIL THE
RIGHT MOMENT.

BUT YOU ONLY
GET ONE LIFE

& YOU DESERVE
TO LIVE IT

FOR REAL.

誠實面對自己也許令人害怕，
也很難做到，
可能需要時間淬鍊等待適當時機。
但我們不過僅此一生，
值得真實地活這麼一回。

APOLOGIZE TO YOURSELF

- SORRY I DIDN'T TRUST YOU
- SORRY I STAYED UP SO LATE

向自己道歉
- 對不起，我沒有相信你
- 對不起，我熬夜熬到很晚

IT'S A BIRTHDAY! THE WORLD IS FULL
OF PEOPLE CELEBRATING EVERY DAY.

DRAW AN EXTRA CANDLE EACH TIME
YOU'RE HERE, THEN BLOW THEM ALL
OUT WHEN <u>YOUR</u> BIRTHDAY COMES.

生日快樂！這個世界上，每天都有無數人在
慶祝生日。

每次翻到這一頁，都畫一根蠟燭吧，等到你
過生日時，再來把這些蠟燭通通吹熄。

REPEAT AFTER ME:

IF I CAN'T BE "AMAZING," I'LL BE "~~FUCK~~ING AMAZING" INSTEAD.

跟著我念：
如果我不是「超棒」，
那肯定就是「棒透了」。

_____

_____

_____

_____

_____

_____

DRAW YOUR LAST MEAL:

畫下你的上一餐：

 NOW 現在

 LATER 下一餐

 AGAIN 再一餐

 SOON 接著呢

DESSERT 甜點

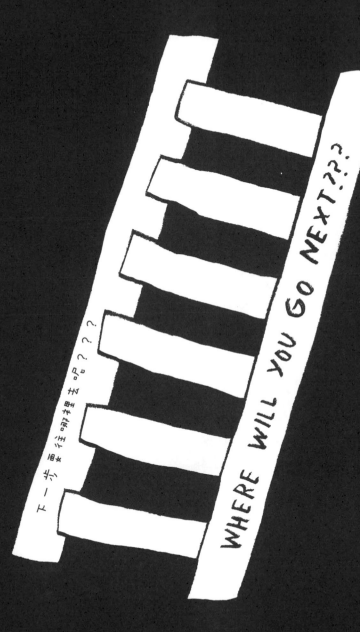

THE WORLD IS
BIG & I AM NOT
BUT I AM STILL
ENOUGH

世界很大，
而我很渺小，
但我就是最好的我

FIND A BONE TO PICK THEN <u>BURY</u> IT!
挑一根骨頭，然後把它埋了！

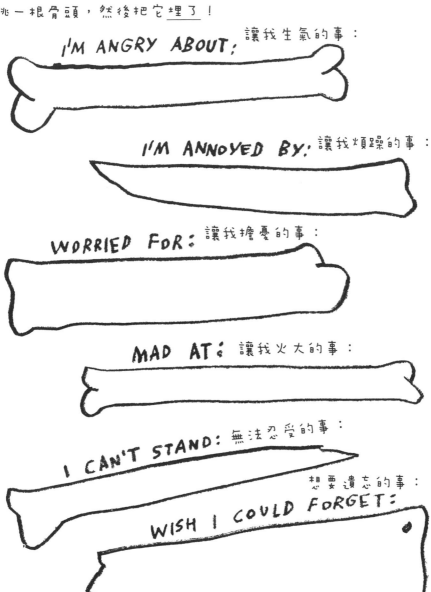

I'M ANGRY ABOUT: 讓我生氣的事：

I'M ANNOYED BY: 讓我煩躁的事：

WORRIED FOR: 讓我擔憂的事：

MAD AT: 讓我火大的事：

I CAN'T STAND: 無法忍受的事：

想要遺忘的事：
WISH I COULD FORGET:

我們要永遠陪伴彼此哦!

POST & TAG YOUR BFF
#PICKMEUPBOOK

發文並標記你一輩子的知心好友
#改寫自己的命運之書

WHAT CAN YOU BUILD WITH A SMALL STEP NOW?

只是一小步的話，你現在能建立什麼呢？

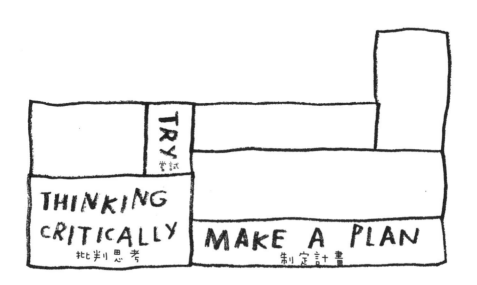

TRY
嘗試

THINKING CRITICALLY
批判思考

MAKE A PLAN
制定計畫

每個人總有一天都會離開這個世
界，所以盡情享受這段旅程吧。
做個善良的人，發揮正面影響
力，或是去吃一塊餅乾吧。

EVERYONE HAS TO GO
SOMEDAY SO WE JUST
HAVE TO ENJOY THE
JOURNEY. BE A GOOD
PERSON, MAKE
POSITIVE CHANGE,
& MAYBE HAVE
A COOKIE.

晚點聊

ULTIMATE BUCKET LIST

FILL THE LIST WITH YOUR DREAM ACTIVITIES OR
ACHIEVEMENTS, THEN PUT IT INTO THE WORLD

人生願望清單

列出你夢想中的活動或目標，然後分享出去，

讓全世界都看到

1 _____

2 _____

3 _____

4 _____

5 _____

6 _____

7 _____

8 _____

9 _____

10 _____

#PICKMEUPBOOK

DRAW A SLICE OF BREAD.
DRAW A TOASTER.
COME BACK SOON OR
YOU'RE BURNT TOAST!

畫一片麵包，
再畫一台烤麵包機。
快點回來哦，不然吐司就要烤焦了！

HELLO?　　　哈囉？

HI?　　　你好？

SORRY,　　真遺憾，

YOU'RE　　你失戀啦！

BREAKING

UP!

TEAR & CRUMPLE THIS
PAGE BIT BY BIT

一點一點地把這一頁撕下來
揉成一團吧

IT'S A VERY STRANGE TIME
TO BE ALIVE, WHEN WE
CAN SHARE PRIVATE IDEAS
& FEELINGS INSTANTLY,
ON THE INTERNET.

REMEMBER THAT LIKES,
NOTES, FAVES & SHARES
ARE JUST NUMBERS &
DON'T LET THAT GET TO
YOU. SURE, WE ALL LIKE
TO BE HEARD, BUT WHEN
EVERYONE'S SHOUTING
AT ONCE, IT ALL SORT OF
GETS A BIT LOST.

我們活在一個多麼奇妙的時代，
隨時都可以透過網路分享個人的想法和心情。

那些按讚、留言、訂閱和分享都只不過是數字
而已，可別讓它們影響你。的確，我們都喜歡
得到關注，但如果眾聲喧嘩，很容易就讓人迷
失其中了。

你知道嗎：

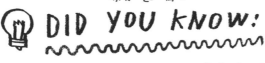 DID YOU KNOW:
〜〜〜〜〜〜〜〜〜〜〜

- HARD WORK CAN PAY OFF
- LOVE IS ACTUALLY REAL
- DEATH IS INEVITABLE

• 努力會有收穫
• 愛真實存在
• 死亡無可避免

TAKE A DEEP BREATH.
HOLD FOR THREE SECONDS,
THEN EXHALE BELOW:

深吸一口氣，
保持三秒鐘，
然後對著下圖呼氣：

BREATHE
HERE
在此呼氣

TAKE A CHILL PILL.
DRAW SOME TO TAKE LATER.

吃一顆定心丸，
再多畫幾顆，以備不時之需。

若說眼睛是靈魂之窗，
請記得把張貼的布告都看過。

IF OUR EYES ARE THE
WINDOWS TO THE SOUL,
MAKE SURE TO READ
ANY POSTED SIGNS.

HELP
WANTED
———
INQUIRE
WITHIN

HELP
YOUR
SELF

幫自己一把

需要幫助，
入內詢問

PLEASE NOTE:
請注意：

WATCH
YOUR
STEP!
當心腳下！

WRITE SOMETHING TO WORK ON OR GROW THROUGH RIGHT NOW:

現在寫下一些你值得做，或能讓你有所成長的事：

NOW _____
現在

LATER _____
之後翻到這頁

NEXT TIME _____
下一次

AGAIN _____
再一次

SOON _____
又一次

SOMETIME _____
日後翻到時

ONCE MORE _____
再度翻到

I AM TRYING
VERY HARD TO
DISAPPEAR
    RIGHT NOW,
 PLEASE GO TO
      ANOTHER   PAGE

我巴不得馬上消失不見，
請翻到別頁吧

CELEBRATE EVERYTHING!

大肆慶祝！

WHAT CAN YOU CELEBRATE TODAY?

今天有什麼值得慶祝的事嗎？

KEEP CLIMBING ON & UP
(MAYBE ADD A HANDRAIL)

不斷往上爬
（也許需要加個扶手）

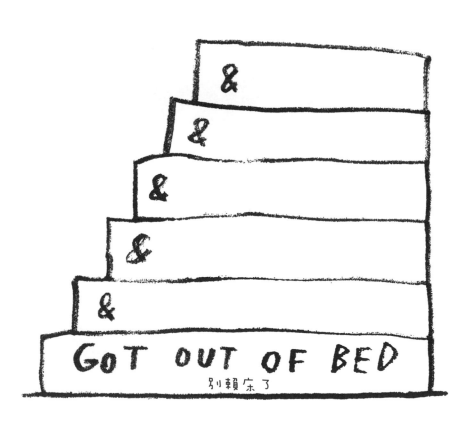

WHAT'S A RECENT ACCOMPLISHMENT YOU NEVER THOUGHT WAS POSSIBLE?

最近實現了哪些以前總認為不可能達成的目標？

NOW _____
現在

LATER _____
之後翻到這頁

NEXT TIME _____
下一次

AGAIN _____
再一次

SOON _____
又一次

SOMETIME _____
日後翻到時

ONCE MORE _____
再度翻到

THERE'S SOMETHING SPECIAL
ABOUT BEING ALONE IN ANOTHER
PLACE. IF YOU'VE BEEN FEELING
A LITTLE WEIRD, MAYBE GIVE
YOURSELF TIME FOR A SOLO
JOURNEY. NONE OF THAT
"EAT PRAY LOVE" STUFF,
JUST TIME TO REMEMBER
YOUR BASIC INSTINCTS.

OKAY, MAYBE YOU
SHOULD EAT SOMETHING
THOUGH.

獨自一人身處異地是種特別的體驗，
如果你感到有點不對勁，或許該來場
獨自旅行。不必像《享受吧！一個人
的旅行》（Eat, Pray, Love）那樣，
只要花些時間好好跟自己相處，喚醒
初心。

好啦，旅程中美食也是必須的。

ADD A COMMENT WITH EACH VISIT, THEN TRY TO NEVER READ THEM AGAIN!

每次翻到這頁時都留下一些話，
絕不要回頭看之前寫的！

DRAW COFFEE CUPS, EACH SHAKIER THAN THE LAST:

畫幾杯咖啡，
每一杯都比前一杯
更搖搖欲墜：

情緒有時並不理性，
那就寫下來吧，
現在不用擔心該如何
處理它們。

EMOTIONS AREN'T
ALWAYS RATIONAL
SO JUST WRITE THEM
DOWN & DON'T WORRY
ABOUT EXPLAINING
THEM RIGHT NOW.

WHAT COULD GO WRONG:

可能遇到的問題：

WHAT ACTUALLY HAPPENED:

實際發生的事情：

CONNECT THE DOGS:

把這些狗狗連起來：

AHH! SORRY, I MEANT DOTS!
F~~UCKING~~ AUTOCORRECT!!

啊！抱歉，是把「點」連起來才對！
該死的自動校正功能！！

EMOTIONAL BREAKDOWN

情緒崩潰

HOW DO YOU FEEL?

你感覺如何？

WHY? 為什麼？

HOW LONG? 多久了？

WHO KNOWS? 有誰知道？

WILL THIS LAST?

這種感覺會持續下去嗎？

會 YES

NO 不會

HOW WILL YOU HANDLE IT?

該如何處理？

FORGET ABOUT IT! 就忘了吧！

TODAY'S DATE: _____

今天的日期：

ENJOY THE UNKNOWN

享受未知

WHILE YOU STILL CAN

趁還活著

SMART

聰明鬼

CURRENT BEST FRIEND:
現在最要好的朋友：

DATE _____ FRIEND _____

DATE _____ FRIEND _____

DATE _____ FRIEND _____

DATE _____ FRIEND _____

DATE _____ FRIEND _____

DATE _____ FRIEND _____

DATE _____ FRIEND _____

DATE _____ FRIEND _____

DATE _____ FRIEND _____

DATE _____ FRIEND _____

日期   好友

COUNT YOUR BLESSINGS
& WATCH THEM PILE UP

數數你擁有的福氣
看著它們越堆越高吧

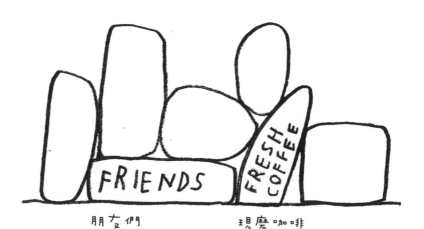

朋友們　　　　現磨咖啡

MAYBE YOU'RE NOT AS ALONE AS YOU THOUGHT

也許你沒有想像中那麼孤單

THE INTERNET IS DETACHED, BUT PEOPLE ARE REAL

網路冷漠疏離，但人是真實的

WE ARE ALL CONNECTED

我們全都與彼此相連

SHARE ANY TIME #PICKMEUPBOOK

隨時分享#改寫自己的命運之書

HAVE YOU EVER HAD YOUR HEART BROKEN?
IT'S REALLY JUST PROOF THAT LOVE IS
REAL, AND OUT THERE! OF COURSE THERE
WILL BE PLENTY MORE TO COME.

IF IT'S BEEN A WHILE, YOU MIGHT BE
STARTING TO FORGET. HOLD ON TO
THOSE MOMENTS WHEN LOVE WAS
UNDENIABLE, EVEN IF THEY'RE KIND
OF BITTERSWEET NOW.

TIME IS LIKE A THREAD. A STITCH IS
NOT VERY STRONG, BUT MANY STITCHES
CAN MEND ANYTHING. SEW OR DRAW A
NEW STITCH NOW & ADD MORE LATER.

你有過心碎的感覺嗎？心碎證明了你曾經真的愛
過！當然，之後也許還會經歷更多次心碎。

過了一段時間後，可能會漸漸開始遺忘，這時候
回想起過往甜蜜，心還是會酸酸的，但還是要牢
牢記住那些愛真實存在的時刻。

時間就像針線，縫一針還不太牢固，但多縫幾針
就能修補一切。現在就來縫上或畫下一個新的線
跡吧，之後每次翻到這頁時再加上更多。

WHAT'S YOUR (CURRENT) GREATEST CHALLENGE?

你（目前）面臨最大的挑戰是什麼？

NOW _____
現在

LATER _____
之後翻到這頁

NEXT TIME _____
下一次

AGAIN _____
再一次

SOON _____
又一次

SOMETIME _____
日後翻到時

ONCE MORE _____
再度翻到

DRAW A STRAW IN A TOUGH SITUATION & SUCK IT UP!

選一個裝了逆境的杯子，在裡頭畫根吸管，然後把它們通通喝光！

※附註：原文中「Suck it up」有「別抱怨，做就對了」的意思。

諸事不順　　　心煩氣躁

烏雲密布

WRITE THANK-YOU NOTES TO YOURSELF

寫下給自己的感謝便利貼

THANK YOU FOR
謝謝你，因為

I APPRECIATE
我很感激

MAN, YOU REALLY
天啊，你真是

THANKS AGAIN
再次感謝

IT MEANT A LOT WHEN
對我意義重大

A TOKEN OF MY GRATITUDE
送個謝禮給你

OKAY, THANKS, LOVE YOU!!

好啦，就是很感謝，愛你哦！！

QUICK, COVER YOUR SCREEN BEFORE YOUR BOSS SEES!

快趁老闆看到之前遮住電腦螢幕！

DRAW YOUR
CURRENT SELF:

畫下自己現在的模樣：

NOW	現在

LATER	之後翻到這頁

AGAIN	再一次

SOON	又一次

HOW (NOT) TO LIVE A FULFILLING LIFE

- COMPARE YOURSELF TO OTHERS REGULARLY

- OBSESS ABOUT ALL THE THINGS THAT CAN GO WRONG

- QUESTION THE MOTIVES OF THOSE WHO LOVE YOU & PUSH THEM AWAY

- <u>NEVER</u> PLAN AHEAD

- IGNORE YOUR BODY & MIND WHEN THEY GIVE YOU WARNING SIGNS

- EXPECT EVERYTHING WHILE GIVING NOTHING

如何（不）過得完滿充實

- 常常拿自己和別人比較

- 總是擔心事情都會出錯

- 懷疑那些愛你的人的動機，
  把他們推得遠遠的

- <u>從不</u>事先計畫

- 無視身體和心理發出的警訊

- 不願付出，只想不勞而獲

THE FIRST THOUGHT YOU HAD TODAY:
今天醒來的第一個念頭：

NOW _____
現在

LATER _____
之後翻到這頁

NEXT TIME _____
下一次

AGAIN _____
再一次

SOON _____
又一次

SOMETIME _____
日後翻到時

ONCE MORE _____
再度翻到

CROSS OUT SOME NEGATIVITY ANY TIME YOU'RE HERE

每次翻到這一頁，就劃掉一些「負面能量」

NEGATIVITY NEGATIVITY NEGATIVITY
NEGATIVITY NEGATIVITY NEGATIVITY
NEGATIVITY NEGATIVITY NEGATIVITY
NEGATIVITY NEGATIVITY NEGATIVITY
NEGATIVITY NEGATIVITY NEGATIVITY
NEGATIVITY NEGATIVITY NEGATIVITY
NEGATIVITY NEGATIVITY NEGATIVITY
NEGATIVITY NEGATIVITY NEGATIVITY
NEGATIVITY NEGATIVITY NEGATIVITY
NEGATIVITY NEGATIVITY NEGATIVITY
NEGATIVITY NEGATIVITY NEGATIVITY
NEGATIVITY NEGATIVITY NEGATIVITY
NEGATIVITY NEGATIVITY NEGATIVITY
NEGATIVITY NEGATIVITY NEGATIVITY
NEGATIVITY NEGATIVITY NEGATIVITY
NEGATIVITY NEGATIVITY NEGATIVITY

負面能量

DRAW THE DEEP END, THEN DIVE RIGHT IN.

畫一個深水游泳池，馬上跳進去吧！

※附註：「Deep end」除了指游泳池的深水區，也有「困境」的意思。

EVERYONE LEAVES
  EVENTUALLY.
DRAW MORE & WATCH
YOUR FOREST GROW.

人最終都會如葉子般凋零落去。
多畫幾片葉子，看著你的森林繁
茂生長。

※附註：「Leaves」同時有「樹葉」
和「離開」這兩種含義。

DESCRIBE LAST NIGHT'S DREAM IN 3 WORDS:

用三個詞形容昨晚的夢境：

_____ _____ _____

_____ _____ _____

_____ _____ _____

_____ _____ _____

_____ _____ _____

_____ _____ _____

_____ _____ _____

_____ _____ _____

_____ _____ _____

YOU'VE BEEN SENT A RAY OF SUNSHINE!

FORWARD THIS PAGE TO FIVE PEOPLE NOW & ALL YOUR DAYS WILL BE FULL OF LOVE & LIGHT.

IF YOU IGNORE THIS, BE WARNED, LITERALLY NOTHING WILL HAPPEN- BUT YOU'RE NOT A VERY THOUGHTFUL FRIEND, ARE YOU??

一縷陽光溫暖著你！

快把這一頁轉發給五個人，你每天都會充滿愛與光亮哦！

小心了，如果沒有轉發⋯⋯說真的也不會怎麼樣，但你就不算是個貼心的朋友了，對吧？？

WHERE TO NEXT?

接下來要去哪裡呢？

"IMPOSSIBLE" CHALLENGES

挑戰「不可能的任務」

MEMORIES

回憶

FOUNDATION

根本

DRAW YOURSELF AS MUCH EXTRA HELP AS YOU NEED:

畫下你需要的額外幫助，畫越多越好：

DECISION MAKER

決策輪盤

SPIN A PENCIL ON THIS PAGE TO FIND YOUR ANSWER!!!

拿一枝鉛筆放在輪盤上旋轉，找到你的答案！！！

OF COURSE FAILURE IS AN OPTION
DON'T BE RIDICULOUS IT'S LIKE
ONE OF TWO MAIN OPTIONS
& ALSO IT'S GONNA BE FINE.

失敗也是在所難免的嘛，別傻了，事情本
來就有成功和失敗兩種可能，不過一切都
會好轉的。

"HOME" CAN BE A PLACE,
A PERSON, OR SOMETHING ELSE.
WHAT FEELS LIKE HOME NOW?

「家」可以是一個地方、一個人或別的事物。
什麼會讓你有家的感覺呢?

NOW _____
現在

LATER _____
之後翻到這頁

NEXT TIME _____
下一次

AGAIN _____
再一次

SOON _____
又一次

SOMETIME _____
日後翻到時

ONCE MORE _____
再度翻到

DRAW YOUR FAVORITE BOOK:
畫下你最愛的書：

NoW
現在

LATER
之後翻到這頁

AGAIN
再一次

SOON
又翻到了

DISAPPEAR (FROM THE INTERNET) FOR A DAY. SHARE HERE INSTEAD & POST THIS PAGE LATER.

試試（從網路上）消失一天，想分享什麼就記錄在這，之後再把這一頁拍照上傳。

📷 #PICKMEUPBOOK

EVERYTHING

所有

YOU

你

ELSE

其他

WRITE A SECRET
ENCOURAGEMENT
FOR THE FUTURE.
DON'T SHARE THIS!

悄悄寫一段鼓勵的話給未來的自己。
這部分就別與人分享了！

HOW DO YOU FEEL TODAY?

你今天心情如何？

請勿打擾：

每當翻到這一頁，就把書闔上。
靜靜地坐一會兒。

SOMETIMES YOU JUST HAVE TO WAIT.

有時候，你只是需要耐心等待。

INSECURITY
IS LIKE A PRECIOUS
TREASURE
TO INSPIRE &
MOTIVATE, SO BURY
THAT ~~SHIT~~ DEEP
& DON'T TELL
EVERYONE
ABOUT IT.

不安全感
有如珍貴的寶藏，
能帶給我們靈感與動力，
就把這種感覺深深埋藏心中吧，
可別跟任何人說啦。

THINK ABOUT EVERYTHING THAT YOU DIDN'T KNOW YOU COULD DO, UNTIL YOU DID IT ANYWAY.

START A LIST & ADD AS YOU RETURN.

有沒有哪些你原先以為自己辦不到，最後
卻還是做到了的事情。把這些事列下來
吧，以後如果翻到這一頁時再慢慢添加。

_____   _____

_____   _____

_____   _____

_____   _____

_____   _____

_____   _____

_____   _____

_____   _____

_____   _____

_____   _____

SORRY

I JUST DO
NOT
CARE AT ALL

不好意思
我根本一點都不在乎

POST THIS ANY TIME
YOU LITERALLY CANNOT

你無言以對時，
就把上圖發布出去吧

#PICKMEUPBOOK

WHAT'S SOMETHING YOU CAN IMPROVE ON??

你有什麼需要改進的地方？

NOW _____
現在

LATER _____
之後翻到這頁

NEXT TIME _____
下一次

AGAIN _____
再一次

SOON _____
又一次

SOMETIME _____
日後翻到時

ONCE MORE _____
再度翻到

YOUR TRUE MOTIVATION
MAY BE INTANGIBLE,
BUT MAYBE SEEING
THIS PAGE FROM TIME
TO TIME WILL BE A
USEFUL REMINDER
TO STAY FOCUSED ON
YOUR GOALS & DREAMS.

你真正的動力
往往難以捉摸，
但也許時不時
看看這一頁，
會提醒你要專注朝著
自己的目標和夢想前進。

CHECK SOMETHING OFF YOUR LIST:
把完成的事項一一打勾：

IT'S SO SATISFYING!
很有滿足感吧！

A BLANK PAGE CAN BE
TERRIFYING, SO FILL THIS
PAGE IN BIT BY BIT
WHENEVER YOU'RE HERE.

整整一頁空白會讓人發慌，
那就一點一滴地把這一頁填滿吧。

I KNOW

YOU

SLEEP

BUT LIKE,

DO YOU

EVEN

DREAM,

BRO??

我知道
你
會睡覺，
不過，
你會不會
做夢呢，
老兄？？

OKAY, WHAT'S YOUR EXCUSE THIS TIME ??

好啦，這次你又有什麼藉口了？？

NOW _____
現在

LATER _____
之後翻到這頁

NEXT TIME _____
下一次

AGAIN _____
再一次

SOON _____
又一次

SOMETIME _____
日後翻到時

ONCE MORE _____
再度翻到

PUT A TINY VOICE IN EACH HEAD:

在每個腦袋裡，放進一個小小的聲音吧：

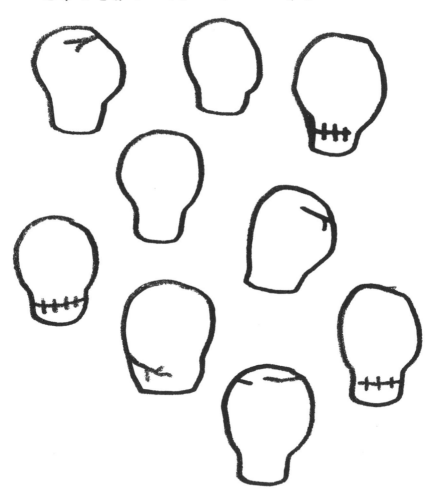

DRAW SOMETHING GREAT SO YOU CAN COME BACK & BE ALL PROUD OR WHATEVER

畫些厲害的東西，這樣下次回來看到時，你會為此感到自豪的

I'M DEAD

我凋謝了

YOU'RE NOT
(CHEER UP)

而你還活著
（振作點呀！）

WHAT ARE YOU AFRAID OF?
WRITE ONE THING NOW, THEN
FACE IT NEXT TIME & ADD ANOTHER!
你在害怕什麼？
先寫下一件害怕的事，好好面對之後，
下次再繼續寫其他事！

_____

_____

(OKAY NOW FACE IT)（來吧，面對它）

_____

_____

(STARE IT DOWN)（直視恐懼）

_____

_____

(DEAL WITH IT)（好好處理）

_____

_____

(YOU GOT THIS)（你可以的）

_____

_____

(WHAT FEAR? YOU'RE INVINCIBLE!!!)
（有什麼好怕的？你無人能敵！！！）

EMERGENCY
EXIT

緊急出口

LET'S GET OUT
OF HERE!

我們快離開這裡吧！

DRAW A MAP OF YOUR FRIEND'S HOUSE.
MARK THEM WITH AN "X" SO YOU
CAN TREASURE THEM FOREVER.

畫一張你朋友家的地圖。
用「X」標記出他們的位置，就可以一輩子珍惜他們啦。

KNOW YOUR WORTH
KNOW YOUR VALUE

STOP TRYING TO IMPRESS
OR CONVINCE SOMEONE
WHO DOESN'T CARE.
FOCUS ON THE PEOPLE WHO
ARE WILLING, ABLE &
RECEPTIVE. YOU CAN'T
WASTE TIME ON SOMEONE
WHO DOESN'T LOVE OR
RESPECT YOU. DO YOUR
THING & LET THE REST
HAPPEN (OR NOT).

COME BACK ANY TIME YOU
NEED TO READ THIS AGAIN.

知道自己的價值

與其不斷向那些不在乎你的人證明自己的價值，
不如把心力花在願意幫助你並接受你的人身上。
別再浪費時間應付那些不愛你也不尊重你的人。
做好自己的本分，其他的事情就順其自然吧。

有需要的時候，隨時都可以回來讀讀這段話。

WRITE YOUR UNPOPULAR OPINIONS, THEN KEEP THEM TO YOURSELF!

寫下一些與眾不同的觀點，
不用讓別人知道！

- FRENCH FRIES ARE GROSS
- I HATE TO RELAX

- 炸薯條真噁心
- 我討厭休息放鬆

PLANT YOUR GARDEN:

栽種你的花園：

EMOTION BINGO

情緒賓果遊戲

LOVE 愛	DIS-APPOINTMENT 沮喪	ABLE 充滿力量	CALM 冷靜	LOVED 被愛
ENJOY-MENT 愉快	ANXIOUS 焦慮	WORRY 擔憂	ANGER 生氣	WONDER 驚奇
APPRE-CIATION 感謝	GREAT 棒透了	FREE SPACE 自由自在	CONTENT 滿足	BRAVE 勇敢
SATIS-FIED 滿意	TRUST 信任	FEAR 害怕	FRUST-RATION 挫敗	REST-LESS 不安
CURIOUS 好奇	EXCITE-MENT 興奮	PEACE 平靜	ENCOU-RAGED 受鼓舞	JOY 喜悅

MARK A CURRENT FEELING ANY TIME YOU'RE ON THIS PAGE. FIVE IN A ROW WINS!

每當翻到這一頁時，把當下的心情圈起來。
只要五個連成一條線就贏了！

LIFE IS UNPREDICTABLE
BUT PATTERNS FORM

生活難以預測
但仍有跡可循

GOALS FOR THIS YEAR

今年的目標

ERROR 404:

THE PAGE COULD NOT BE DISPLAYED

錯誤訊息：
無法顯示頁面

DRAW A NEW DOOR EACH TIME SO YOU CAN GET OUT OF HERE!

每次翻到這一頁就畫一扇門，
好讓你逃離這裡！

EXIT 出口

OKAY, SO LIKE,
WHAT DOES
"LIVE LIKE YOU'RE DYING"
EVEN MEAN?

OF COURSE YOU'RE DYING,
WE ALL ARE, BUT
PROBABLY NOT TOMORROW
SO WHY SPEND TODAY
"LIVING" FRANTICALLY?

好啦，真搞不懂
「把每一天都當成生命中的最後一天」
到底是什麼意思。

當然，我們都在走向死亡，這是免不了的，
但通常不太可能明天就死，
所以為什麼要把今天「活得」那麼瘋狂呢？

THERE IS SO MUCH TO BE
GRATEFUL FOR!
WRITE ONE THING NOW &
ADD MORE LATER.

值得感謝的人事物太多了！
現在先寫下一件事，
之後再慢慢加上更多。

HEY! HERE'S AN IDEA:
MAYBE TRY TO
LOWER YOUR
EXPECTATIONS &
ENJOY WHAT YOU
HAVE??

嘿！給個建議：
也許可以試著少些期待，
享受現在所擁有的？？

DRAW SOMETHING UNREMARKABLE.
NEXT TIME GIVE IT SOME MAGIC!

畫一些平凡小物。

下次翻到這頁，再為這些東西施點魔法吧！

EMOTIONAL BREAKDOWN

情緒崩潰

HOW DO YOU FEEL?

你感覺如何？

WHY?
為什麼？

HOW LONG?
多久了？

WHO KNOWS?
有誰知道？

WILL THIS LAST?

這種感覺會持續下去嗎？

會 **YES**

NO 不會

HOW WILL YOU HANDLE IT?

該如何處理？

FORGET ABOUT IT! 就忘了吧！

TODAY'S DATE: _____

今天的日期：

FIND YOUR WAY THROUGH THE DARK

在黑暗中找到自己的路

OKAY

沒問題了

TAPE A #5 BILL
TO THIS PAGE TO
SPEND ON YOUR
FIFTH VISIT HERE

只要翻到這頁就貼一張百元鈔票，
集滿五張就把這些錢通通花掉

TREAT COUNTDOWN:
歡樂倒數：

□ □ □ □ □
5 4 3 2 1

HALF-FULL OR HALF-EMPTY?

杯子是半滿，還是半空呢？

※附註：悲觀的人看到杯子裡面有半杯水，會說：「只剩下半杯水了。」；樂觀的人則會說：「還有半杯水耶！」

FEELING BAD?
THERE'S AN APP FOR THAT!

心情不好嗎？
試試這些應用程式吧！

WHAT'S SOMETHING STUPID YOU'VE CAUGHT YOURSELF DOING RECENTLY?

你最近有做了什麼蠢事嗎?

NOW _____
現在

LATER _____
之後翻到這頁

NEXT TIME _____
下一次

AGAIN _____
再一次

SOON _____
又一次

SOMETIME _____
日後翻到時

ONCE MORE _____
再度翻到

LET YOUR MIND CLEAR FULLY.
FOCUS ONLY ON YOUR
BREATHING & FLOAT AWAY
FOR A WHILE. WHEN YOU
COME BACK HERE, YOU'LL
KNOW WHAT TO DO.

將腦袋完全淨空。
只專注於你的呼吸,
讓思緒飄得遠遠的。
當你把注意力拉回到這裡時,
你就會知道該怎麼做了。

DRAW GOOD-LUCK CHARMS, THEN CUT THEM OUT AS NEEDED:

畫一些幸運符，
有需要的話，把它們剪下來隨身攜帶：

INCREASE YOUR
ENGAGEMENT BY
AFFIXING TO
YOUR BUTT:

在屁股上貼這張紙來增加互動：

PLEASE
FOLLOW
BACK

來互追互讚吧

#PICKMEUPBOOK

THINGS I CAN FOCUS ON

我把心思放在

- STAYING POSITIVE
- TANGIBLE ACCOMPLISHMENTS
- SELECT INTANGIBLE ACCOMPLISHMENTS
- BEING A DECENT PERSON

- 保持樂觀
- 實現具體成就
- 學會放棄不切實際的目標
- 做個體面的人

THINGS I CAN NOT FOCUS ON

不把心思放在

- NEGATIVITY
- SELF—DOUBT
- THINGS BEYOND MY CONTROL
- ANY OF YOUR BULL~~SHIT~~

- 悲觀負面
- 自我懷疑
- 自己掌控不了的事
- 你那些狗屁倒灶的事

MEET YOUR MATCH:

遇見你的火柴 :

IT'S NOT BIG, EXPENSIVE OR MODERN, BUT IT CAN CREATE GREAT CHANGE FOR BETTER OR WORSE.

IT'S NOT UNIQUE, BUT RATHER ONE OF MANY, AND YET IF USED WELL, THIS ONE MIGHT BURN THE LONGEST & BRIGHTEST OF ALL.

雖然它小小的、不高檔也不時髦，
但能帶來巨大的改變，無論這改變是好是壞。

它不是獨一無二，而是千千萬萬火柴中的一根，
但如果運用得當，將能點燃最長久、最奪目的光芒。

WHENEVER YOU'RE HERE
FIND A DARK PLACE
TO COLLECT YOUR THOUGHTS,
THEN WRITE ONE DOWN:

每當你來到這一頁，
找一個暗處好好沉澱一下，再把想法寫下來：

DRAW YOUR GUTS, THEN TRY TO TRUST THEM.

畫出你的直覺，
就跟著感覺走吧。

I DON'T
KNOW WHY
THIS EXISTS
BUT I'M
GLAD IT DOES.

我不知道這頁存在的原因，
但我還是很高興有它的存在。

THERE'S A FINE LINE BETWEEN JEALOUSY & INSPIRATION. HOW CAN YOU GROW FROM THIS FEELING?

嫉妒和受激勵往往只有一線之隔，
如何讓這種情緒幫助你成長呢？

WRITE A TINY WISH THEN GLUE IT FACEDOWN ON THE PAGE. KEEP ON MAKING WISHES!

寫下一個小小的願望，
然後把寫有心願的那一面朝下，
貼在這一頁。持續許願吧！

DRAW YOURSELF NOW
畫下現在的你

SEEMINGLY IMPOSSIBLE CHALLENGE
看起來是不可能完成的挑戰

THEN DO IT AGAIN LATER
之後再畫一次吧

A WORD
YOU'VE NEVER TRULY
UNDERSTOOD BEFORE:

你從沒真正理解的詞語：

_____   _____

_____   _____

_____   _____

_____   _____

_____   _____

_____   _____

_____   _____

_____   _____

_____   _____

_____   _____

ONE "YES" LEADS TO ANOTHER!
ADD MORE WHEN YOU'RE HERE.

一個「肯定」會為你帶來更多的肯定！
每次來到這一頁，就再多肯定自己一些吧。

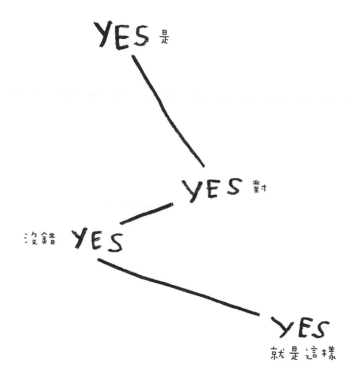

YES 是

YES 對

沒錯 YES

YES
就是這樣

YOU CAN BE YOUR
OWN SUPPORT
SYSTEM

你可以做自己的強力後盾

CARRY YOURSELF
WITH DIGNITY
& COMPASSION

保有自尊和惻隱之心

& REMEMBER TO LIFT
WITH YOUR LEGS,
NOT YOUR BACK

記得別用錯方法而傷了自己

TEAR A SMALL PIECE OF THIS
PAGE TO CARRY WITH YOU.
TAKE A LITTLE MORE NEXT
TIME TOO. ENJOY FEELING
CONNECTED TO THE REST OF
YOUR THOUGHTS IN THIS BOOK.

從這一頁撕下一小角帶在身邊，
下次再撕一點隨身帶著，
享受與這本書有所連結的感覺。

DRAW YOUR BODY &
LABEL YOUR INNER STRENGTHS:

畫下自己的身體，
標出你的內在力量：

#SELFIE #PICKMEUPBOOK
#自拍 #改寫自己的命運之書

YOU CAN
GO FORWARD

你可以前進

BUT NOT
BACK

但無法後退

BECAUSE
LIFE MOVES
ON

因為生活還在繼續

WHETHER
YOU'RE READY

無論你準備好了

OR NOT

還是沒有

DON'T BE AFRAID
TO SPEAK UP.
IF NOBODY CAN
HEAR YOU, HOW
WILL THEY

別害怕說得大聲一點。
如果大家都聽不見你說話，
又怎麼會注意聽你說了什麼？？

LISTEN??

傾聽？？

WRITE YOURSELF A LETTER
NOW, THEN FOLD THE PAGE
& MARK A DATE TO OPEN
IT IN THE FUTURE.

寫一封信給自己，然後把這一頁摺起來，
定一個未來的日期，到時重新打開它。

KEEP ON SCROLLING
繼續翻頁吧

NOTHING TO SEE HERE
這裡沒什麼好看的

NO MATTER WHERE YOU ARE,
GREAT THINGS ARE HAPPENING
AROUND YOU. SOMEONE'S KID
JUST SPOKE FOR THE FIRST
TIME. OLD FRIENDS ARE
REUNITING. IF THIS ISN'T
YOU TODAY, TOMORROW MIGHT
BE YOUR TURN FOR
    SOMETHING
        WONDERFUL.

無論你在哪裡，身邊都會有好事發生，
可能是某個人的寶寶第一次開口說話，
或是與老朋友重逢。
如果你今天過得不好，也許明天好事就會
輪到你了。

WRITE YOUR PROBLEMS IN PENCIL NOW, THEN ERASE THEM OVER TIME UNTIL YOU'RE IN THE CLEAR.

用鉛筆寫下你目前遇到的麻煩，等問題解決了再擦掉，直到這一頁重新變回空白。

WRITE A MESSAGE IN A BOTTLE
THEN CUT IT OUT & FLOAT IT AWAY
(DRAW MORE BOTTLES AS NEEDED)

在瓶子裡寫一段話，
然後剪下瓶子，隨水漂流而去
（若有需要，可以多畫一些瓶子）

DRAW SOME
LABELS, THEN
DON'T APPLY
THEM TO YOURSELF.

畫一些標籤，
可別對號入座了。

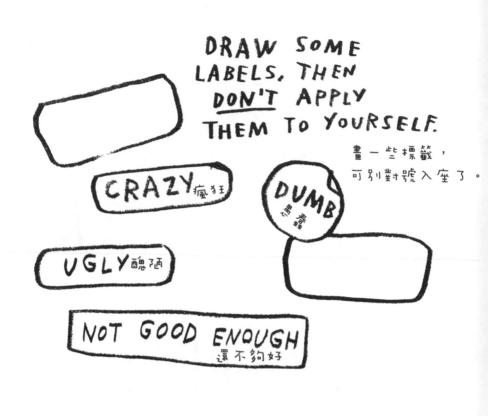

CRAZY 瘋狂

DUMB 愚蠢

UGLY 醜陋

NOT GOOD ENOUGH
還不夠好

PILE UP YOUR ANXIETIES
THEN KNOCK THEM DOWN:
層層堆疊起你的焦慮
然後再一舉推倒：

FEELING UNCOOL
感覺自己太落伍

SUSPICION OF
INADEQUACY 總懷疑準
備不充分

THERE ARE
SO MANY PEOPLE
IN THE WORLD & THEY
ALL HAVE BIG & SMALL
PROBLEMS & IT CAN
BE HELPFUL TO
REMEMBER THAT
LIFE IS JUST A
SERIES OF TASKS &
CHALLENGES &
MOMENTS &
FEELINGS FOR
EACH OF US.

世界上許許多多的
人，都面臨著大大
小小的問題，而我
們每個人或許都該
記住，人生不過是
由一連串的考驗、
挑戰、某種時刻和
感受累積而成。

MIDNIGHT THOUGHTS:
午夜思緒：

#PICKMEUPBOOK

IT CAN BE HARD
TO COMMUNICATE
SOMETIMES. TRY TO
REMEMBER THAT
EVERYONE IS
DIFFERENT, LIKE
SNOWFLAKES.

(IF SNOWFLAKES HAD
BRAINS THAT
PROCESSED THE WORLD
& THEIR EXPERIENCES
IN VASTLY DIFFERENT
WAYS.)

有時候會覺得難以溝通，
那是因為每個人都如雪花般獨一無二。

（如果雪花也有思想，能對世界有所認知，
那麼每片雪花的感受也會大有不同吧。）

IT'S NICE THAT WE CAN BLAME THE MOON
FOR ALL OUR CRAZY EMOTIONS & BEHAVIOR!
能把我們的情緒失控和瘋狂行為全都推給月亮真是
太好了！

CURRENT MOON: _____ ◯
現在的月相：
MADE ME: _____
所以我表現出：

_____

_____

CURRENT MOON: _____ ◯
現在的月相：
MADE ME: _____
所以我表現出：

_____

_____

CURRENT MOON: _____ ◯
現在的月相：
MADE ME: _____
所以我表現出：

_____

_____

START HERE
& DRAW LOOPS
AROUND IN A
SINGLE,
SMOOTH
ACTION-

REPEAT
WHENEVER.

從這裡開始，
一筆畫出流暢線條的圈。
隨時都可以再來畫圈哦。

LOVE THIS PAGE,
THEN GIVE IT AWAY,
PIECE BY PIECE.

給這一頁滿滿的愛，
然後一點一點把愛分送出去吧。

THINK ABOUT
WHAT YOU REALLY
WANT. TURN IT
OVER IN YOUR
MIND. HOLD THE
THOUGHT. VISUALIZE
IT FULLY.

NOW SNAP OUT
OF IT!! THIS IS
REAL LIFE.

SET ACTIONABLE
STEPS TOWARD
YOUR GOAL,
THEN ~~FUCKING~~
DO SOMETHING.

想想你真正想要的是什麼，
在心中反覆思索，
記住這個想法，好好想像一下。

快醒醒啊！！回到現實生活。

為目標設定具體可行的步驟，
然後就做點什麼吧。

LETTING GO IS HARD.

放下很難

PRACTICE BY PUTTING THIS BOOK DOWN FOR A BIT & MAYBE DOING SOMETHING ELSE.

就先練習把這本書放下一會兒吧，
也許可以去做些別的事情。

YOU MADE IT
TO THE LUCKIEST
PAGE IN THE BOOK!
THIS IS A GOOD SIGN.
HAVE A GREAT DAY!

你翻到了本書最幸運的一頁！
這是個好兆頭。
祝你有美好的一天！

MAKE A MESS NOW
& DIG YOURSELF OUT LATER:

先 來 製 造 點 混 亂 吧，
之 後 再 慢 慢 收 拾 ：

OKAY 好吧

BUT 但是

THAT 這種

SINKING 下沉的

FEELING 預感

MIGHT 可能

HAVE 是

A 真的

POINT 有問題啊

HAVE A PERSONAL BREAKTHROUGH

做一件自我突破的事

WRITE ABOUT YOUR PAST NOW, THEN ADD MORE LATER. WHEN THE PAGE IS FULL, TEAR THROUGH!

寫寫你過去所做的突破，每次回到這裡都寫一些，等到整頁都寫滿了，就把這一頁撕下來！

DRAW OVER A MISTAKE
TO MAKE SOMETHING NEW:

在每個錯誤上塗塗改改，
創造出嶄新的模樣：

SOMETIMES YOU JUST WANT
TO SCREAM & CRY BUT
YOU CAN'T. OTHER TIMES
YOU TOTALLY CAN!

FIND YOURSELF A SAFE,
PRIVATE SPACE TO
LET IT OUT. YOU ARE
AN <u>AMAZING</u> &

<u>EMOTIONAL</u> PERSON

WHO <u>FEELS</u> FEELINGS.

THIS CAN BE ANNOYING
SOMETIMES BUT IT'S
ALSO YOUR SECRET POWER.

KEEP BEING HUMAN.

有些時候你只是想要放聲大哭，
但你不能這麼做，
不過其他時候，你完全可以！

為自己找一個安全的私人空間，宣洩出來。
你是個心思細膩又情感豐沛的人，
能感受到各種情緒。

這樣的特質有時候很煩，
但同時也是你的祕密武器之一。
繼續做個感性的人吧。

WHAT DOES <u>YOUR</u> MILK SHAKE BRING TO THE YARD?

你的奶昔為你帶來了什麼？

※附註：應該是出自Kelis 的〈Milkshake〉這首歌，裡面有一句歌詞「My milkshake brings all the boys to the yard我的奶昔把全部的男生都招來院子裡」，大家對於「奶昔」的意思各有解讀，可以是自己與眾不同的特點。

☐ BOYS
男孩

☐ GIRLS
女孩

☐ GENDER IS A CONSTRUCT
社會所建構的性別

☐ FRIENDS
朋友

☐ BRAIN FREEZE
透心涼

☐ DIABETES
糖尿病

☐ #THIRST
口渴

☐ COPYRIGHT LAWYERS
版權律師

☐ POSITIVE AFFIRMATION
正面肯定

☐ DROUGHT (NATURE'S THIRST)
乾旱（大自然口渴了）

☐ COWS/HORSES
母牛／馬

☐ TOURISTS
旅行者

☐ TULIPS
鬱金香

☐ MORE MILK SHAKES
更多奶昔

☐ THE BEATING OF HIS HIDEOUS HEART
他劇烈的心跳聲

PLANNING AHEAD IS ITS OWN REWARD. WHAT'S YOUR PLAN FOR TODAY?

預先規劃會讓你事半功倍。
你今天有什麼計畫？

NOW _____
現在

LATER _____
之後翻到這頁

NEXT TIME _____
下一次

AGAIN _____
再一次

SOON _____
又一次

SOMETIME _____
日後翻到時

ONCE MORE _____
再度翻到

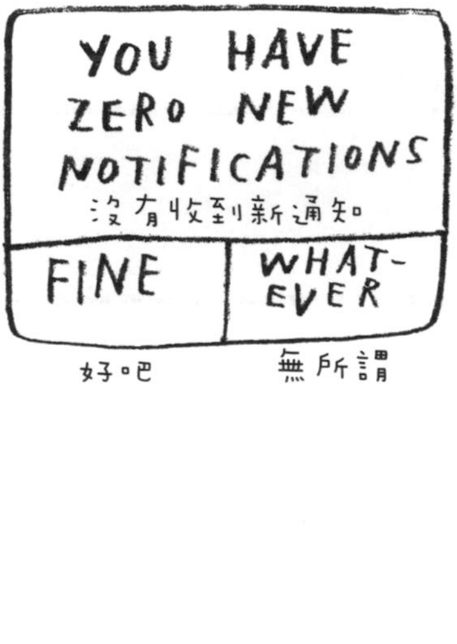
YOU HAVE ZERO NEW NOTIFICATIONS
沒有收到新通知
FINE
WHAT-EVER
好吧
無所謂

DRAW A MOLD, THEN PRACTICE NOT FITTING INTO IT.

畫一個模子，然後練習不照著模子走。

※附註：fit the mold 有「勉強自己適應環境」的意思。

請幫幫忙！
其實也沒什麼特別的事啦，
只是想知道有沒有人會看到。

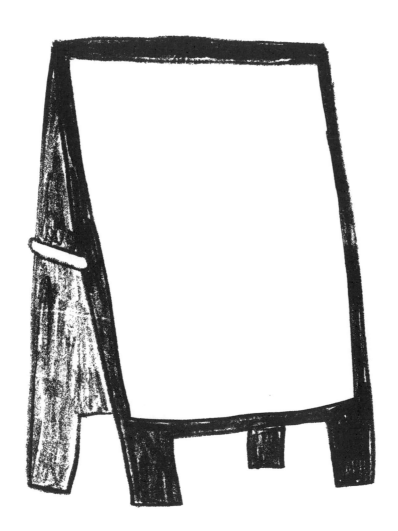

YOU HAVE READ 10/10
FREE PAGES THIS MONTH
→ SUBSCRIBE NOW ←

你已經把本月的免費頁面全看完了

立即訂閱

DRAW A MOTIVATIONAL POSTER

畫一張能激勵你的海報

NOW POST IT! #PICKMEUPBOOK

現在發出去！#改寫自己的命運之書

THIS IS ONLY A MIRROR WHEN IT'S TURNED OFF

關機之後，這就只是一面鏡子了

WHAT'S YOUR FAVORITE SONG RIGHT NOW?

你現在最愛哪一首歌呢？

SONG: _____   SONG: _____
ARTIST: _____   ARTIST: _____
DATE: _____   DATE: _____

SONG: _____   SONG: _____
ARTIST: _____   ARTIST: _____
DATE: _____   DATE: _____

SONG: _____   SONG: _____
ARTIST: _____   ARTIST: _____
DATE: _____   DATE: _____

SONG: _____   SONG: _____
ARTIST: _____   ARTIST: _____
DATE: _____   DATE: _____

SONG: _____   SONG: _____
ARTIST: _____   ARTIST: _____
DATE: _____   DATE: _____

SONG: _____   SONG: _____
ARTIST: _____   ARTIST: _____
DATE: _____   DATE: _____

（歌曲／歌手／日期）

SHARE YOUR PLAYLIST WITH #PICKMEUPBOOK WHEN IT'S FULL
全部填完之後，拍照上傳並加上#改寫自己的命運之書標
籤，把你的歌單分享給大家

ROCK BEATS
SCISSORS,
BUT PAPER
WINS EVERY
TIME

石頭贏剪刀，但出
布總能無往不利

GIVE SOMEONE YOUR NUMBER

把電話號碼給某個人

CALL ME SOMETIME:

記得打給我：

YOU'RE A TOTAL BABE:

寶貝隨時打給我哦：

TEXT ME AS LATE AS YOU WANT:

無論多晚都可以傳訊息給我：

I'M SPEECHLESS NOW, CALL ME LATER:

我現在不想說話，晚點再打：

DID IT HURT WHEN YOU FELL FROM HEAVEN?
你從天堂掉下來痛不痛？

※附註：Did it hurt when you fell from heaven是一句老套的搭訕用語，藉此稱讚對方就像落入凡間的天使。

PROPOSED MANTRAS

- IT'S TOO BAD "COOL" IS A SOCIAL CONSTRUCT BECAUSE I AM PRETTY COOL

- ~~IF AT FIRST YOU DON'T SUCED~~

- PLEASE PASS THE CHOCOLATE

- I CAN DO ANYTHING IF I JUST PUT IT TO MY FOREHEAD & APPLY PRESSURE

- I AM DEFINITELY WORTH FOLLOWING ONLINE

- TO THINE SELFIE BE TRUE

精神喊話一下

- 我超酷啊，可惜「酷」這個詞是由社會所建構出來的概念
- ~~如果一次不成~~
- 請把巧克力遞過來
- 如果把目標貼在額頭上，施加一點壓力，我就什麼都做得到了
- 我絕對值得在網路上受到關注
- 自拍要拍出自己真實的模樣

WORK AROUND
THE OBSTACLES

遇到障礙不妨繞道而行

POST THIS PAGE & TAG SOMEONE FOR EACH BOX. COLOR IT IN FIRST!

在你的社交平台上分享這一頁，
每一格標記一個好友。先把每一格都塗上顏色吧！

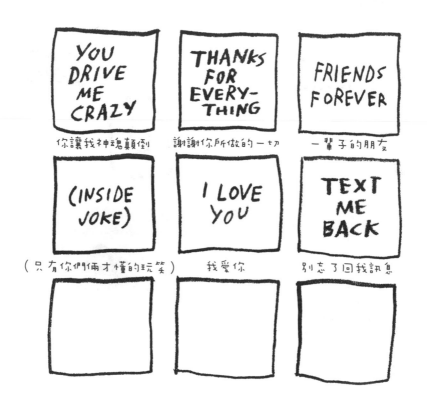

YOU DRIVE ME CRAZY
你讓我神魂顛倒

THANKS FOR EVERY-THING
謝謝你所做的一切

FRIENDS FOREVER
一輩子的朋友

(INSIDE JOKE)
(只有你們倆才懂的玩笑)

I LOVE YOU
我愛你

TEXT ME BACK
別忘了回我訊息

(FILL IN THE BLANKS!) #PICKMEUPBOOK
（填滿其他空格！）#改寫自己的命運之書

WHERE ARE YOU RIGHT NOW?

你現在在哪裡?

TIME _____
PLACE _____

TIME _____
PLACE _____

TIME _____
PLACE _____

TIME _____
PLACE _____

TIME _____
PLACE _____

TIME _____
PLACE _____

TIME _____
PLACE _____

TIME _____
PLACE _____

TIME _____
PLACE _____

TIME _____
PLACE _____

TIME _____
PLACE _____

TIME _____
PLACE _____

(時間/地點)

DO YOU EVER
FEEL LIKE
YOU HAVE
NO IDEA
WHAT YOU'RE
DOING???

SAME.
I THINK IT'S
NORMAL &
PROBABLY
OKAY.

你是否有過不知道
自己在幹嘛的時候？？？

我也有過，迷惘是人之常情吧，
沒關係的。

RIGHT NOW I AM 我現在

_____

BUT I'D RATHER BE 不過我想

_____

THIS TIME I'M 這次我

_____

BUT I'D RATHER BE 但我更想

_____

UGH, I'M SO 唉，我真的很

_____

I WISH I WAS 如果當時我

_____

CURRENTLY 目前

_____

CAN I PLEASE 希望我能

_____

WHAT IS WRONG WITH YOU???

你到底是怎麼了啊？？？

(SERIOUSLY, WRITE SOMETHING THAT'S NOT GREAT, THEN CROSS IT OUT NEXT TIME IF IT'S BETTER.)

（說真的，寫下一些煩心的事情吧，如果下次來到這一頁時，情況有好轉了再把它劃掉。）

EMOTIONAL BREAKDOWN

情緒崩潰

HOW DO YOU FEEL?

你感覺如何？

[ ]

WHY?
為什麼？

[ ]

HOW LONG?
多久了？

[ ]

WHO KNOWS?
有誰知道？

[ ]

WILL THIS LAST?
這種感覺會持續下去嗎？

會 (YES)   (NO) 不會

HOW WILL YOU HANDLE IT?
該如何處理？

FORGET ABOUT IT!
就忘了吧！

[ ]

TODAY'S DATE: _____
今天的日期：

NEVER
GIVING UP
IS HOW YOU
WIN.

永不放棄，勝利就會是你的。

SOMETHING YOU REALLY REALLY REALLY WANT RIGHT NOW:

你現在超級無敵想要的東西：

NOW _____
現在

LATER _____
之後翻到這頁

NEXT TIME _____
下一次

AGAIN _____
再一次

SOON _____
又一次

SOMETIME _____
日後翻到時

ONCE MORE _____
再度翻到

POWER's OUT!
筋疲力盡！

BETTER RECHARGE
好好充個電吧

WHAT'S IN YOUR CUP?
杯子裡裝了什麼?

GOAL TO ACCOMPLISH BEFORE THE NEXT TIME YOU RETURN TO THIS PAGE:

下次回到這一頁前，你想要達成的目標：

DID YOU DO IT? ☐ YES ☐ NO

你做到了嗎？　☐是　☐否

REGULAR EGGS
CRACK & RUN
BUT NEST EGGS
APPRECIATE OVER TIME

一般的雞蛋容易被打碎或丟失,但巢裡的雞蛋會隨著時間,越來越有價值

※附註:nest egg 除了指「巢裡的蛋」,還有「儲蓄、儲備金」的意思。

LIFE IS TOO SHORT TO PUT UP WITH PEOPLE WHO DON'T TREAT YOU WELL.

人生短暫，不必忍耐那些對你不好的人。

STICK UP FOR YOUR-SELF. BE YOUR OWN BIGGEST SUPPORTER.

為自己出頭，做自己最大的靠山。

YOU ARE WORTH IT.

這是你的價值所在。

YOU DESERVE THIS.

這是你應得的。

NEVER FORGET IT.

千萬不要忘記。

NAVIGATE THROUGH YOUR OWN DARKNESS
穿越黑暗，尋找出路
YOU CAN
你可以的
YOU WILL
你會找到
YOU DID
你做到了

WRITE ONE NICE THING ABOUT YOURSELF WHENEVER YOU'RE ON THIS PAGE

每次翻到這一頁，
就寫下自己的一個優點

_____   _____

_____   _____

_____   _____

_____   _____

_____   _____

_____   _____

_____   _____

_____   _____

_____   _____

_____   _____

_____   _____

WHAT'S THE NICEST THING SOMEONE HAS SAID TO YOU LATELY? ADD IT TO THE LIST!

最近別人對你說過最溫暖好聽的話是什麼？
把這些話寫在下面吧！

NOW _____
現在

LATER _____
之後翻到這頁

NEXT TIME _____
下一次

AGAIN _____
再一次

SOON _____
又一次

SOMETIME _____
日後翻到時

ONCE MORE _____
再度翻到

WRITE A TINY SECRET, THEN TEAR
IT OUT & HIDE IT. DO IT AGAIN & AGAIN
UNTIL THIS PAGE HAS DISAPPEARED.

寫下一個小祕密，然後把它撕下來藏好，
每次都重複這麼做，直到這一頁完全消失不見。

I DON'T KNOW
WHERE YOU ARE
NOW BUT I AM
IN THE PAST,
THINKING ABOUT
YOUR FUTURE,
& I HOPE THAT
YOU ARE HAPPY.

我不知道你現在身處何方，
而我身處過去，想著你的
未來，希望你幸福快樂。

_____   _____

_____   _____

_____   _____

_____   _____

_____   _____

_____   _____

_____   _____

_____   _____

_____

_____   **WHAT DO**
                            YOU THINK
_____   **WILL**
                            HAPPEN
_____   **NExT?**

_____   你認為接下來會
                            發生什麼呢?

NEED SOME
ALONE TIME?
需要一點獨處的時間嗎？

COVER YOURSELF
IN MIRRORS TO
APPEAR AS A
SHIMMERING
MIRAGE TO
PASSERSBY.

躲在鏡子背後，
對來往的行人來說，
你就像閃著微光的海市蜃樓。

WRITE SOMETHING REALLY HONEST
THEN PRESS THE PAGE TO YOUR FACE
& FEEL THE WEIGHT OF YOUR TRUTH.

寫下一些對自己坦誠的話，
然後把這一頁按在臉上，
感受真實的重量。

THINGS CAN'T JUST
GO BACK TO "HOW THEY WERE"
BECAUSE THERE IS NO BACK
& THERE NEVER CAN BE.
LIFE ONLY MOVES FORWARD.

STOP TRYING TO GO BACK
OR YOU WILL ALWAYS BE
DISAPPOINTED.
YOU WILL NEVER READ THIS
FOR THE FIRST TIME AGAIN.

FOLD THIS PAGE SHUT.
YOU CAN REVISIT IT,
BUT IT'S ALREADY
A MEMORY.

事情不可能回到「從前的樣子」，因為時光無法倒流，也回不去了，生活只會不斷向前。

別再頻頻回頭，不然往往只會換來失望。
你永遠不會再和第一次閱讀這段話時有相同感受。

闔上這本書，你當然可以再次翻到這裡，但對這一頁的想法已成往事了。

A NAGGING THOUGHT YOU CAN'T GET OUT OF YOUR HEAD TODAY

你今天揮之不去的小煩惱

NOW _____
現在

LATER _____
之後翻到這頁

NEXT TIME _____
下一次

AGAIN _____
再一次

SOON _____
又一次

SOMETIME _____
日後翻到時

ONCE MORE _____
再度翻到

WHO THE ~~FUCK~~ DO YOU
THINK YOU ARE??
ANSWER NOW, AGAIN
LATER, & TRACK YOUR
CHANGES.

你以為你是誰？？
寫下你現在的答案，
之後再回答一次，
看看自己的轉變。

BOOKS I'VE CLAIMED TO HAVE READ:

我聲稱自己讀過的書：

_____

_____

_____

_____

_____

_____

_____

讓我們坐在這裡，攤開這一頁

LET'S JUST SIT HERE
& HOLD THIS PAGE
WITHOUT TALKING

靜默不語

WHAT ARE YOU GOOD AT?
WHAT MIGHT YOUR PURPOSE BE?
ADD ONE THING EACH VISIT
UNTIL THE PAGE IS USE-FULL!

你擅長什麼？ 你要怎麼發揮所長呢？
每當翻到這頁，就寫下一件事，
慢慢把這整頁寫得滿滿的！（會對你很有幫助哦）

TAPE A PHOTO OF YOURSELF HERE & STARE YOURSELF DOWN

在這裡貼一張你的相片，好好看看自己

WRITE A SECRET THAT YOU SHOULDN'T TELL.
CHANGE ALL THE DETAILS. CROSS IT OUT.
DESTROY THE PAGE. OKAY, MAYBE JUST
 DON'T DO ANYTHING TO BEGIN WITH.

寫下一個你不能說的秘密。
改掉所有的細節、通通劃掉，再把這一頁撕毀。
好吧，也許一開始根本就不該寫出來。

OH GOOD!
HERE'S THAT SHORTCUT
YOU WERE LOOKING FOR

太棒了！
這就是你一直在找的捷徑

DRAW YOUR MIND
THEN LOSE IT: 畫下你的想法，
再把它忘掉：

DRAW A PIZZA.
ADD A TOPPING WHENEVER
YOU'RE HERE, THEN
   ORDER IT FOR REAL
    AFTER THE FIFTH TIME!

畫一個披薩。
每次回到這頁就加上一種配料，
集滿五種就真的去點一個來吃吧！

SOMETHING YOU DID THAT MIGHT HAVE BEEN BAD BUT YOU DIDN'T REALIZE IT AT THE TIME:

你曾做過什麼很糟糕，但你當時沒有察覺到的事：

_____

_____

_____

_____

_____

_____

_____

SOMETHING YOU'D LIKE BUT WOULD NEVER BUY FOR YOURSELF:

你很喜歡但絕對買不下手的東西:

TODAY 現在
_____

NEXT TIME 之後翻到這頁
_____

LATER 下一次
_____

KEEP GOING 繼續寫
_____

_____

_____

_____

_____

_____

_____

_____

_____

_____

_____

(NOW TREAT YOURSELF FROM THIS LIST!)
(現在就以這張清單開始犒賞自己吧)

TEXT THIS PAGE
TO A FRIEND
WHENEVER YOU
LAND HERE.
MAKE IT EXTRA
COOL FIRST!

每次你來到這裡，就把這一頁傳給一個朋友。
不過要先讓這一頁變得酷一點吧！

SLOWLY FILL THIS PAGE
WITH POSITIVE THOUGHTS,
THEN SHARE WHEN IT'S FULL

慢慢用各種正面樂觀的想法填滿這一頁，
填滿之後再分享出去

_____   _____

_____   _____

_____   _____

_____   _____

_____   _____

_____   _____

_____   _____

_____   _____

_____   _____

_____   _____

#PICKMEUPBOOK

SOMETHING I NEED TO REMEMBER:

一些我需要記住的事情：

DRAW YOURSELF
A BLANK REALITY
CHECK FOR LATER.

畫一張真正的空白支票
給未來的自己。

WRITE A SECRET MOTIVATION
ON THE BOTTOM OF YOUR
SHOE & THEN HIT THE
GROUND RUNNING!

在鞋底寫下你內心潛藏的動力，
然後盡全力奔跑吧！

HOW TO THROW AN EFFECTIVE TANTRUM

怎麼好好發一頓脾氣

- LOSE YOUR COOL IMMEDIATELY TO ENSURE NOBODY WANTS TO COME NEAR YOU.

- IF SOMEONE DOES TRY TO HELP, SHOUT "YOU DON'T UNDERSTAND!" NOBODY ELSE HAS EVER HAD A BAD DAY BEFORE.

- BREAK SOMETHING YOU OWN. THAT WAY YOU STILL SUFFER EVEN WHEN YOU HAVE CALMED DOWN.

- RANT ONLINE, BECAUSE THERE'S NOTHING QUITE AS SATISFYING AS SELF-SABOTAGE!

- 立即拋棄你所有的冷靜，讓大家離你遠遠的。
- 如果有人來關心你，就對他大吼「你什麼都不懂！」好像除了你以外，沒有人經歷過不順心的日子一樣。
- 亂摔亂砸東西，不過等冷靜下來可是會後悔莫及。
- 上網發洩，沒有什麼比自暴自棄、放肆咒罵更讓人心滿意足的了！

216

GET A SONG
OUT OF YOUR HEAD
BY PUTTING IT HERE:

想擺脫腦海中不斷出現的音樂旋律，
就把這些歌曲寫在這裡吧：

ARTIST:

SONG:

SAMPLE LYRIC:

ARTIST:

SONG:

SAMPLE LYRIC:

ARTIST:

SONG:

SAMPLE LYRIC:

ARTIST:

SONG:

SAMPLE LYRIC:

（歌手／歌曲／歌詞節選）

CHARGE UP THE PAGE UNTIL IT'S FULL:

為這一頁充飽電：

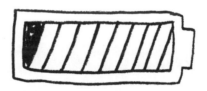

GREAT! YOU HAVE THE POWER TO DO ANYTHING!

很好！現在什麼事都難不倒你了！

WHAT CAN YOU MAKE FROM (ALMOST) NOTHING?

你要怎麼（幾乎）從零開始，從無到有？

ADD SOMETHING NEW NOW
& AGAIN LATER!

每次都加上一些新玩意！

UPDATE YOUR STATUS:
更新你的狀態 :

NOW 現在

LATER 之後翻到這頁

AGAIN 再一次

ONCE MORE 又一次

LOSE YOUR TRAIN OF THOUGHT BY STARTING SOMETHING HERE & CONTINUING ON ANOTHER PAGE.

在這裡開始做些什麼，然後翻到另一頁繼續，
讓思路中斷一下。

WRITE A LIST OF THINGS THAT ARE BAD NOW, THEN CROSS THEM OFF AS THEY BECOME IRRELEVANT

寫下一些現在看起來很糟糕的事，
等這些事變得無關緊要之後就劃掉

GIVE THESE AWAY UNTIL YOU HAVE ZERO Fs TO GIVE!

把這些F通通分送光吧！

OR GIVE THEM ONLINE #PICKMEUPBOOK

或放上網路 #改寫自己的命運之書

A REALLY STRONG, POSITIVE FEELING:

寫下一種十分強烈又正面的感受：

NOW _____
現在

LATER _____
之後翻到這頁

NEXT TIME _____
下一次

AGAIN _____
再一次

SOON _____
又一次

SOMETIME _____
日後翻到時

ONCE MORE _____
再度翻到

COMMEMORATE THE SMALL MOMENTS WITH SOME QUICK LITTLE DRAWINGS:
簡單幾筆畫下這些微小時刻作為紀念：

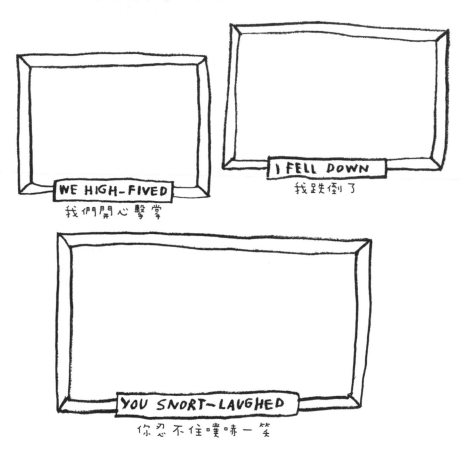

WE HIGH-FIVED
我們開心擊掌

I FELL DOWN
我跌倒了

YOU SNORT-LAUGHED
你忍不住噗哧一笑

SHARE THESE MEMORIES #PICKMEUPBOOK
用#改寫自己的命運之書標籤分享這些回憶

TRY TO DRAW SOMETHING
DIFFICULT, THEN GIVE UP
UNTIL NEXT TIME:

挑戰畫一些高難度的東西，
就算放棄了也沒關係，
留到下次再繼續吧：

FILL THIS SPACE SO YOU'RE NEVER ALONE:

填滿這片空白，你就不再孤單了：

IF THE DOOR
ISN'T LOCKED,
JUST OPEN IT AGAIN!

如果門沒有鎖，就再次打開它！

THE STUPIDEST THING YOU'VE DONE RECENTLY:

你最近做過最愚蠢的事:

NOW _____
現在

LATER _____
之後翻到這頁

NEXT TIME _____
下一次

AGAIN _____
再一次

SOON _____
又一次

SOMETIME _____
日後翻到時

ONCE MORE _____
再度翻到

(IT'S OKAY, WE'RE ALL JUST KIND OF BUMBLING IDIOTS)
(沒事啦,我們多少都犯過傻)

TRY DRAWING SOMETHING NEW:
練習畫一些沒畫過的東西：

A HORSE:
一匹馬：

BUNCH OF BANANAS:
一串香蕉：

MOMENT OF TRUTH:
揭開真相的時刻：

MOUNTAIN TOP:
山頂：

YOUR OWN NOSE:
你的鼻子：

OUTER SPACE:
外太空：

EVERYONE HAS A SOUL MATE, PROBABLY? DRAW THINGS THAT COME IN PAIRS:

每個人應該都有靈魂伴侶吧？
畫一些成雙成對的事物：

WHEN YOU LOOK UP AT THE SKY, WHO ARE YOU THINKING OF?

仰望天空的時候，你會想到誰呢？

WHAT'S AROUND YOU?
DRAW ONE NEARBY THING NOW
& AGAIN LATER UNTIL YOU'RE
COMPLETELY SURROUNDED!

你四周有什麼？
畫出身旁的人事物，每次翻到這一頁都畫一個，
最後讓自己被團團包圍！

DRAW YOUR OWN SUPPORT SYSTEM

畫出支撐你前進的一切

DRAW A SOUVENIR FROM A MOMENT OR <u>FEELING</u>:

為某個瞬間或心情
畫一個紀念品：

悲傷

初吻，1998年

DISGUISE YOUR TERROR BY WRAPPING IT IN OTHER EMOTIONS:

用其他情緒層層包裹，
來掩飾你的恐懼：

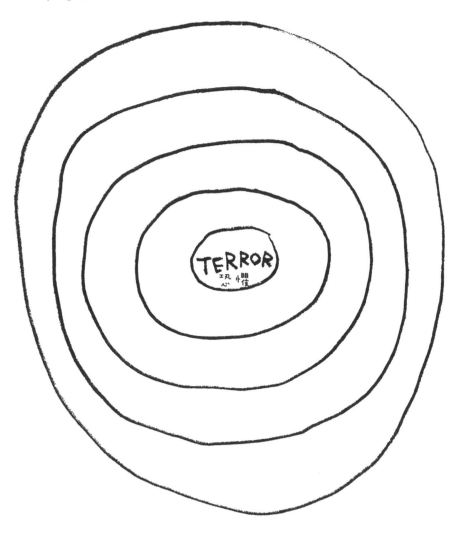

WHAT HAVE YOU ALREADY DONE?

你已經做過哪些事了？

- ☐ ACED A TEST
  考試拿高分
- ☐ BEEN MARRIED
  結婚
- ☐ HAD BREAKFAST
  好好吃頓早餐
- ☐ 100 LIKES
  突破100個讚
- ☐ BRUSHED HAIR
  頭髮做造型
- ☐ CELEB SIGHTING
  親眼見到偶像明星
- ☐ BROKEN BONE
  摔斷骨頭
- ☐ TRUE LOVE
  找到真愛
- ☐ PET A DOLPHIN
  摸摸海豚
- ☐ PLANT A TREE
  種一棵樹
- ☐ DANCE LIKE NOBODY'S WATCHING
  旁若無人地縱情跳舞

- ☐ CRIED ALL NIGHT
  哭一整晚
- ☐ SWIM IN AN OCEAN
  在海裡游泳
- ☐ DRINK 8 CUPS OF WATER
  一天喝8杯水
- ☐ ROLL DOWN A HILL
  滾下山坡
- ☐ LEARN ANOTHER LANGUAGE
  學習新語言
- ☐ GET A TATTOO
  刺青
- ☐ HAVE THE LAST LAUGH
  反敗為勝
- ☐ DANCE LIKE SOMEBODY IS WATCHING
  跳舞時想像有人在旁觀賞

GIVE YOURSELF A TIP:

給自己一點小叮嚀：

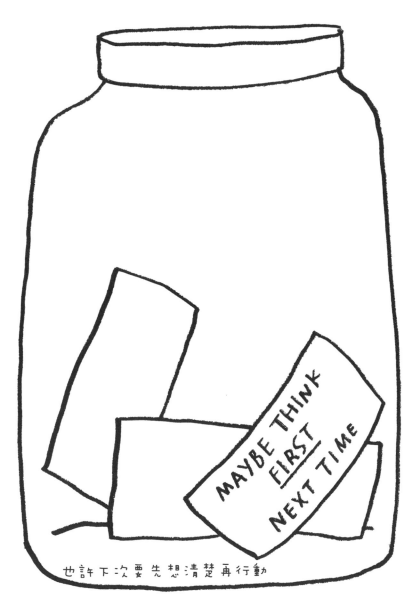

MAYBE THINK FIRST NEXT TIME

也許下次要先想清楚再行動

DRAW THE VEGETABLES
YOU DON'T LIKE, THEN
CROSS THEM OUT AS
YOU GET OVER IT.
(YOU BIG BABY)

畫下你討厭的蔬菜，克服了之後就劃掉。
（你就像個長不大的孩子）

THIS HAPPENED: _____

這件事已經發生了：

_____

BUT IT WAS OKAY BECAUSE: _____

但應該沒什麼關係，因為：

_____

THEN THIS: _____

然後又遇到：

_____

AND IT WAS FINE BECAUSE: _____

現在也解決了，方法是：

_____

& THEN: _____

接著發生了：

_____

BUT: _____

不過：

_____

WHAT ARE SOME THINGS YOU CAN CONTROL? START A LIST NOW & ADD MORE LATER.

什麼是你能掌控的呢？
列出一份清單，每次翻到
這一頁都加上幾項。

WRITE A THANK-YOU NOTE
TO SOMEONE YOU WON'T
SEE AGAIN. PUT IT INTO THE
UNIVERSE WITH #PICKMEUPBOOK!

寫一封感謝信給某個你再也見不到的人，
透過#改寫自己的命運之書讓全宇宙都看到！

THE "WORST" THING ON YOUR CURRENT TO-DO LIST

目前待辦事項中「最難應付」的事情

NOW _____
現在

LATER _____
之後翻到這頁

NEXT TIME _____
下一次

AGAIN _____
再一次

SOON _____
又一次

SOMETIME _____
日後翻到時

ONCE MORE _____
再度翻到

DRAW THE VIEW FROM YOUR WINDOW:

畫出窗外的景色：

RIGHT NOW
現在

KINDA SOON
過一會兒

ANOTHER TIME
又一次

MUCH LATER
很久以後再度翻到

FILL THE PAGE WITH WAVES SLOWLY OVER TIME & STARE AT THEM TO FEEL CALM LATER.

慢慢把這一頁畫滿波浪，
然後凝視這片海浪讓內心平靜下來。

WAVES ALWAYS BREAK BUT THEY NEVER STOP COMING.

就算最後總會碎成浪花，海浪還是不斷奔湧向前。

WHAT DO YOU DO WHEN NOTHING MAKES SENSE?? WHAT OR WHO CAN HELP?

做什麼事都感覺不對勁的時候，你會怎麼辦呢？？
有什麼/誰能幫助你嗎？

THE ANSWER
答案

COME BACK IF YOU FORGET

如果之後忘記了，就回來看看自己當時的答案吧

DRAW A CURRENT EMOTION:

畫出現在的情緒：

STRESSED

壓力好大

THE BEST PART OF YOUR DAY

一天中最美好的時光

NOW _____
現在

LATER _____
之後翻到這頁

NEXT TIME _____
下一次

AGAIN _____
再一次

SOON _____
又一次

SOMETIME _____
日後翻到時

ONCE MORE _____
再度翻到

ANYTHING ✦
CAN BE ✦
SPECIAL IF ✦
YOU CHERISH IT.
✦ WHAT DO
YOU LOVE?

如果懂得珍惜，
一切都會變得特別。
什麼是你心愛且珍視的東西？

EMOTIONAL BREAKDOWN

情緒崩潰

HOW DO YOU FEEL?

你感覺如何？

WHY?
為什麼？

HOW LONG?
多久了？

WHO KNOWS?
有誰知道？

WILL THIS LAST?　這種感覺會持續下去嗎？

會 **YES**

NO 不會

HOW WILL YOU HANDLE IT?
該如何處理？

FORGET ABOUT IT! 就忘了吧！

TODAY'S DATE: _____

今天的日期：

慢慢地用你自己的方式爬上這一頁的頂端

THINGS I'M DEFINITELY GOING TO FORGET, BUT DON'T WANT TO:

那些我肯定會遺忘，但又希望能記住的事：

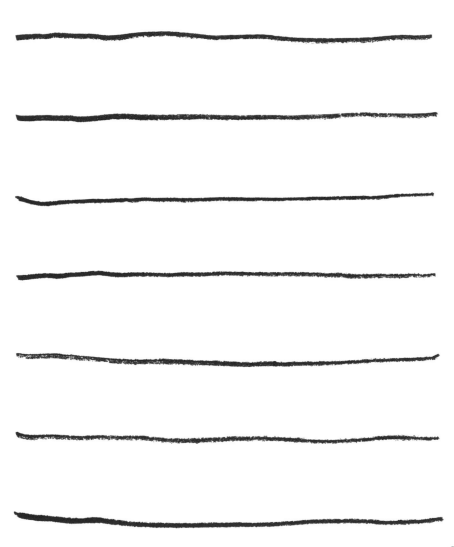

FILL IN YOUR FUTURE!

寫下你嚮往的未來！

預言

PREDICTION

THIS CAN
BE A
MEETING
PLACE

大家有緣相聚

SEE YOU AGAIN SOON

後會有期

THANK YOU:

謝謝你們：

- PENCILS
  鉛筆
- COFFEE
  咖啡
- MITCHELL, JEREMY, TUESDAY, JESSE, HALLIE & SARAH
  米切爾、傑瑞米、特絲緹、傑西、海列、莎拉
- TERROR
  恐懼感
- A CUTE DOG I SAW
  我曾見過的一隻可愛狗狗
- THE INTERNET
  網路
- BRAZIL!!!!!!!
  巴西！！！！！！！
- MARIAN (EDITOR)
  MONIKA (AGENT)
  MYSELF (LOL)
  瑪麗安（編輯）
  莫妮卡（經紀人）
  我自己（笑）